Tranquility Landscapes

Coloring Book

Mandala Mountains, Trees, Forests for
Adults Anti Stress Relaxation

Rachel Mintz

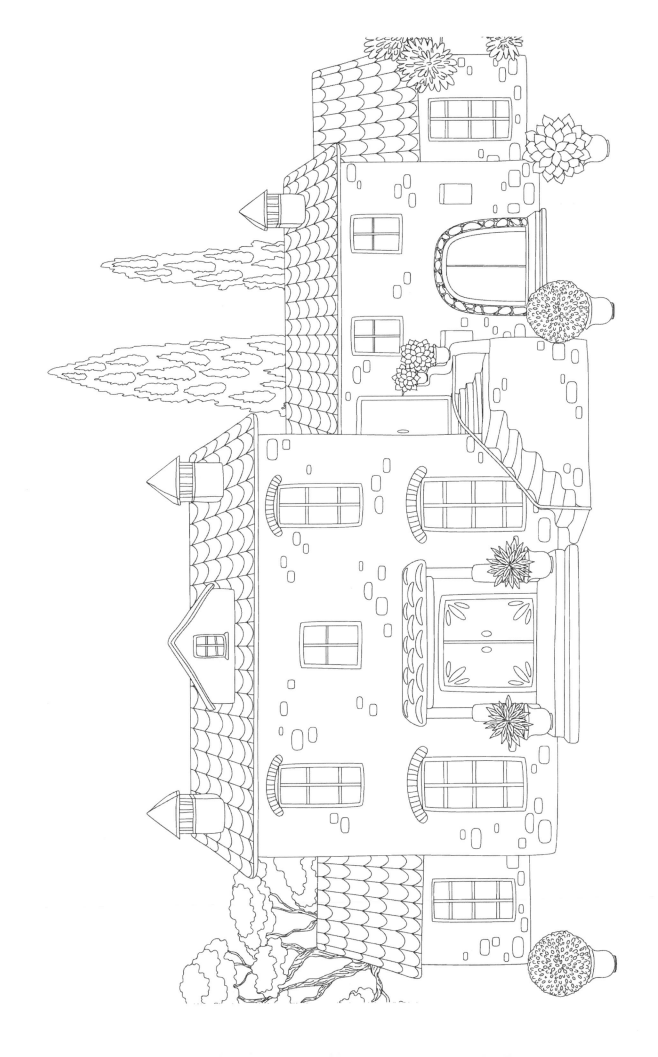

Thank you for coloring with us

Please rate and review this book

More Rachel Mintz coloring books:

Mermaids Heaven
Coloring Book

Rachel Mintz

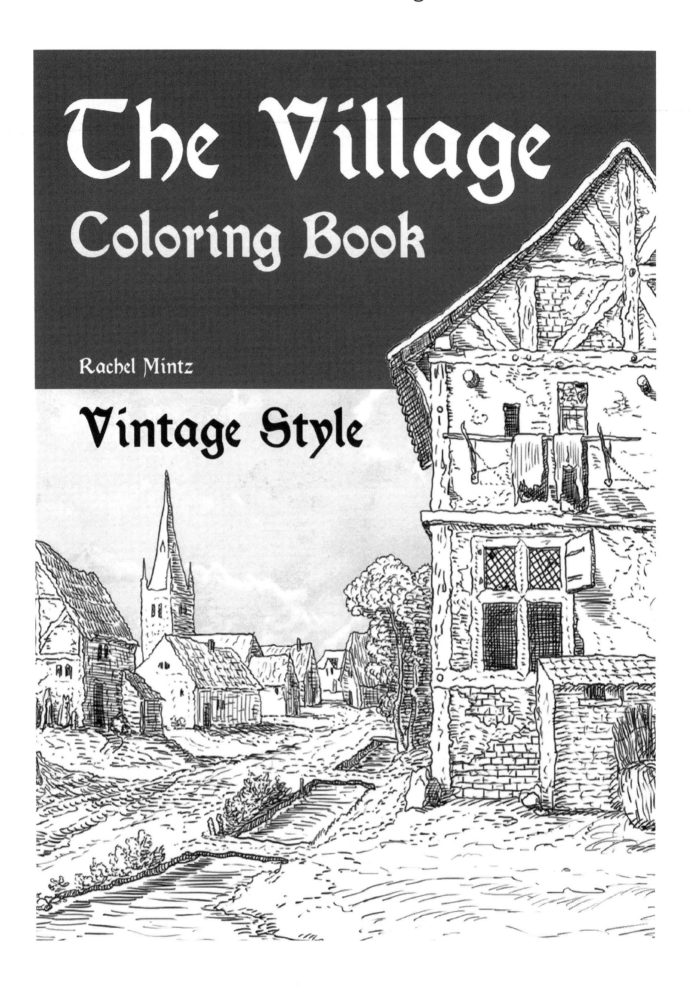

Rachel Mintz

Window Marvels
Stained Glass Coloring Book

Thank you for coloring with us

We will be very thankful if you could take the time to rate & review this book

Made in the USA
Middletown, DE
14 September 2022